IAN HARRIS

2ND EDITION

HOOKED ON YOU

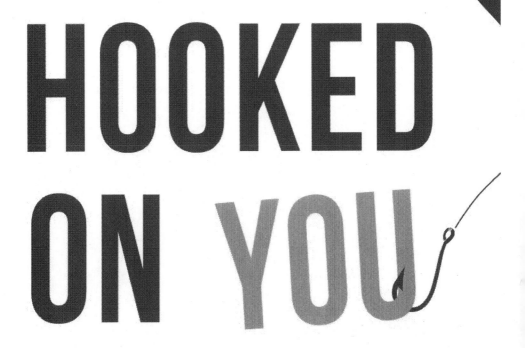

THE GENIUS WAY TO MAKE ANYBODY READ ANYTHING

D0273940

gatehouse

Hooked On You: The Genius Way to Make Anybody Read Anything

Ian Harris

This book is for sale at http://leanpub.com/hookedonyou

This version was published on 2015-01-16

Leanpub

This is a Leanpub book. Leanpub empowers authors and publishers with the Lean Publishing process. Lean Publishing is the act of publishing an in-progress ebook using lightweight tools and many iterations to get reader feedback, pivot until you have the right book and build traction once you do.

Contents

Legal notice 1

About the author 3

Foreword: "Nobody Has to Read This Crap" 5

Why Good Stories Are Great For Business 8

How Stories Make People Read What You Write 15

Where to Find Stories to Hook Your Reader 20
    Non-fiction books 23
    Kindle Popular Highlights 36
    Reddit 42
    Quora 43
    Listening and Tuning In 46

How to Link a Story to Your Message 48
    14 sample bridges 49
    Where to put your bridge 50
    Is your story more important than your message? 54

11 Writing Hacks 56

5 Ways to Write Faster 66

10 Ways to Make Your Writing Look Easy to Read 73

CONTENTS

How to Measure Your Writing 77

Storytelling kit 80

    How to use this storytelling kit 80

    Story 1: NASA 81

    Story 2: Alice in Wonderland 82

    Story 3: KFC 83

    Story 4: Centring the Saltshaker 84

    Story 5: Lobster 85

    Story 6: Ferrari 86

    Story 7: Angry Birds 87

    Story 8: Steve Jobs 87

    Story 9: Finding Nemo 88

    Story 10: Any old map 89

    Story 11: New York 90

    Story 12: Iatrogenesis 91

How to use stories to simplify your presentations 92

Final word 97

Thank you 99

Legal notice

You're on the bus one morning when a tall man takes the seat next to you. He opens his briefcase, takes out some papers and motions for you to remove your headphones:

> "While all attempts have been made to verify information provided in this publication neither the Author nor the Publisher assumes any responsibility for errors, omissions, or contrary interpretation of the subject matter herein."

What? You stare back. Sensing that you're puzzled, the man tries again, more slowly this time:

> "The suggestions outlined within this guide are given in good faith. Neither the Author nor the Publisher assumes any responsibility, financial or otherwise for the way you interpret or use this information and no guarantee is offered on the content herein."

Pleased now, he pauses. But before you can say anything, he discovers a second sheet he'd overlooked. With a 'silly me' gesture, he continues:

> "In no event will Gatehouse Consulting Limited, Ian Harris or his related Partnerships, Corporations, Limited Companies or other Entities, or the Partners, Agents or Employees thereof be liable to you or anyone else for any decision made or action taken in reliance on the information in this book or for any consequential,

special or similar damages, even if advised of the possibility of such damages."

By now some of the other passengers on the bus are staring. You mumble something about your stop being next, and head towards the door.

As you step off, you can see a figure pressing a document against the window as the bus pulls away. Above the traffic you can just make out the words:

"Permission to reproduce or transmit in any form or by any means, electronic or mechanical, including photo-copying or recording, or by any information storage retrieval system, must be obtained from the author Ian Harris."

About the author

- Ian Harris is associate director of Gatehouse, the go-to communication agency
- Ian has (okay look, it's me) I've been invited to speak at London's Google Campus on storytelling and content marketing. I've spoken at Forward Partners on building an audience through content marketing
- I'm the creator of Rockstar Copy, a live 1-day workshop that shows you how to make people read your writing

I hope you find this book useful. If you have any questions I'm happy to help - email me at **i.harris@gatehousegroup.co.uk**

- Gatehouse helps people to engage, motivate and inspire.
- We publish the Journal of Internal Communication, and the popular blog IC World
- Since 2006, we've worked with 25% of FTSE 100 companies. Would you like to join them?

Foreword: "Nobody Has to Read This Crap"

I wrote this book to help you make people read what you write.

Actually, there's more to it than that: I wrote this book because you're not normal. You're not normal because you like to *read*.

Consider this:

- 58% of the US adult population never reads another book after high school
- 80% of US families did not buy or read a book last year
- Most people who buy a book don't get past page 18

Most people find reading a chore.

Dragging their eyes across text is work to be avoided if possible. That's why most of what you write never gets read. At best it's skipped, scanned and skimmed, but it's never absorbed, taken in or understood.

The best writers are supremely aware of this.

You know how Caesar supposedly paid somebody to follow him around whispering: "Remember, you are only mortal"? Well, in the same spirit a writer friend of mine has a sign above her desk:

"Nobody has to read this crap."

She keeps it there to remind herself that, at some point in the last few years, it became okay for readers to ignore the majority of words that cross their path. There's no longer any shame in not reading every email you're sent, or failing to read the agenda before a meeting. "Tutti colpevoli, nessuno colpevole," as the Italian saying goes: "If everyone is guilty, no one is guilty."

Why this has happened isn't beyond the scope of this little book. If you're looking for a convenient scapegoat you could blame information overload, or our increasingly busy lives. You could blame social media, iPhone addiction, Elvis Presley or fluoride in the water. It doesn't make any difference.

All I know is that in the A.D.D. age, if you want to get your writing read - if you want to place your thoughts into another's mind so you can influence them, inform them or get them to buy something – you'd be wise to apply some of the tactics in this book.

You do that, you'll stick out like a toad in a tutu.

Just remember, nobody has to read this crap.

Before we begin, one more thing...

I've spent 15 years working in the media and – in my experience – most writers never grasp how hard it is to get their writing read.

Most writers will never use the methods you're about to learn in this book. You see, writing is long-range warfare. You launch your missiles from 100 miles out at sea, and you never get to really see the impact you make on the recipient.

Most writers prefer it this way. They write their copy and lob it into the world without watching to see how big the crater is – or whether it lands at all. They get paid all the same.

You have to obsess over the impact your writing makes. When you dial in your missile, you're going for the kill.

In this book, I show you how to make anybody read anything. It really boils down to two things:

- How to find **great stories** to get people's attention
- How to **make them relevant** to your audience

Why Good Stories Are Great For Business

> "Here's a little tip I would like to relate, many fish bite if you got good bait." *Source unknown*

Your personality is one of your business's most valuable attention-getting assets.

I want to kick-off by explaining the business benefits of writing in a way that people will want to read.

Remember the charismatic CEOs of the 1980s? Back then, ordinary people were discovering the stock market for the first time and there was a huge appetite for easy-to-understand news stories about business personalities.

The result: a new breed of corporate leader. Founder CEOs like Steve Jobs and Larry Ellison. Everywhere you looked, leaders were motivating followers and bewitching investors.

Today, that's gone. It's a shame, but it's also an opportunity. It's an opportunity because if you're prepared to show a little heart, you can become well-known and admired in your industry – and bring back some of the magic that's been lost.

All you have to do is publish interesting content about the world you love.

This process takes a little time, but when it happens it's irreversible. Another column in a trade magazine. Another newspaper opinion piece. Another piece of LinkedIn thought leadership. At some point, you switch from being a small feature of the landscape to a permanent, natural wonder of your industry.

Storytelling is one of the most reliable ways to become a celebrity in your industry

I use the 'c-word' carefully here.

Writing probably won't make you Jerry Seinfeld famous, but it can make you 'industry famous'. In other words, famous to the segment of people that you need to get in front of.

You don't need to be Gary Vaynerchuck, Perez Hilton or Michael Arrington – with big, mainstream audiences running into the millions. For most people, it's more than enough to 'famous' to the right 100, 1,000, or 10,000 people that you're hoping to do business with. Still famous the way Kevin Spacey is famous, but within a focused community.

> Writing brings credibility, which in turn brings all kinds of opportunity. You become a safe bet rather than an unknown quantity. It opens all kinds of doors that are otherwise locked tight.

Strong stories can make you a leader

Using strong, insightful stories in your writing is a great way to be recognised as a leader.

In the early nineties, Seth Godin joined a small, struggling software company. His job was to turn science fiction novels into computer games.

He was given an aggressive deadline. What he *wasn't* given was enough programmers. Nobody cared about his project. He desperately needed help.

His solution: writing. Seth created a weekly newsletter that highlighted the work of every single person who worked on one of his products. He made photocopies and distributed them by hand across the company. Within a month, six engineers had defected to join his team. Before long, every person in the department was pitching in.

Seth hit his deadline, and his software sold millions of dollars, saving the company. Says Seth:

> "Did engineers switch because of the newsletter? Of course not. They switched for the journey. They wanted to be part of something that mattered."

This happened 20 years ago, but Seth reckons that people still talk about being part of that team today. If you want to rally folks around a cause, there's no better way than writing interesting, engaging content.

Great writing makes people want to work with you

"Oh, I got money for THAT."

People always have money when it's something they want. There's a story in Super System, a famous book by the poker player Doyle Brunson.

One day, a guy named 'Lowball Pete' goes over to his friend Shorty's house.

> "Shorty, I've got to have some money. The baby don't have any food, the rent's due and they're going to throw me out of my house."

Shorty, who's a good friend of Pete's says:

"Well, I understand. Here's $100."

"Thanks Shorty. I'll pay you back as soon as I can."

"No problem Pete. Where are you going now?"

"I'm going over to Al's house, they have a big poker game going right now."

"Well Pete, what difference does that make? How are you going to play?"

"Oh... I've got money for THAT."

You find this all the time in business. Years ago, I had a small video marketing business. I was in negotiations with a big financial trading firm to create and manage their YouTube channel.

I invested hours consulting with them: researching the opportunity, writing proposals, meeting with stakeholders.

I knew they needed it. They told me they need it.

Except: "No budget."

Only, it wasn't true:

- I couldn't help noticing Facebook pictures of the marketing team at a £450 a head charity ball
- Or the Tweet about a new pool table for the office
- I even knew they'd been laying out £300 a month for a fancy satellite broadband system, when the actual dish was still in its box

People always have money when it's something they want. That's never going to change. The question is: for you, is this a problem – or is there a way to make it a competitive advantage?

If there's one thing I know about great writing, it's that it can turn you and your business into a 'want'.

Entertaining writing can make customers chase you

Life's good, and business is more simpler, when customers approach you.

If you can build an audience of people who enjoy reading what you write, a good number of them will eventually become your customers. And it can happen sooner than you'd think.

Recently, a company I'm with won two big clients. Both are worth about £100K in annual revenue. But while winning the first client took weeks of toil, focus and negotiation, the second client reached out and hired us on a handshake.

Let me explain how it went down these two clients.

Things kicked off with the first client when they sent us an RFP inviting us to pitch for a big contract. This RFP came with 9 pages of instructions:

- Please provide CVs and biographies of your entire team – including any contractors you'll use
- Please tell us how your costs break down (i.e. how much profit are you making?)
- Please invest the best part of two weeks creating concepts, mock-ups and writing proposals – with no guarantee of pay-off at all

Right off the bat, it was a 'parent / child' relationship. Still, we eventually won the business. Fine. Now, here's how the second client went down.

One Saturday evening I got a message on LinkedIn from somebody I didn't know called Alastair. He said:

"Ian, I have a project I'd like to discuss with you."

We set up a phone call. The phone call led to a meeting, where he told us about his project. We listened, and gave him a price. "That's fine" he nodded, and we shook hands.

And that was it. We were done in an hour. No bidding, no battling, no beauty parade.

What happened? Why was the second client so much easier? Well, although I'd never heard of Alastair before he had been familiar with me for nearly a year. When I looked at his records he'd been on our email 'warm-up sequence' after he entered his email address underneath an industry article that I'd written.

Every week since then he'd heard from me via a drip-fed email sequence:

- Drip. An interesting story
- Drip. A piece of helpful advice
- Drip. A useful piece of content

Over the course of a few months, a relationship was established. Trust was built. So when he reached out to me on LinkedIn that Saturday evening, he'd already decided. Alastair – and his £100K contract – were ours to lose.

Writing pays a lot better than you'd think.

Writing gets you better clients

It's also worth mentioning that when you work with clients who approach you, they're generally much better clients than ones that you've had to chase. For example the RFP client haggled the bill, changed the brief and rushed the work. In contrast, the 'easy client' was a peach.

Ultimately, yes – both clients were worth having. But all things being equal, isn't it wiser to optimise your business to attract clients who've already picked you?

How Stories Make People Read What You Write

Picture the moment your writing lands in front of your reader.

Usually, you're competing with every distraction under the sun: emails, phone calls, the 40 other tabs in Chrome. How do you cut through?

What I do is this: I take my message and tie it to a little story. Something interesting and unusual.

I want the reader to feel like they've been dropped into a little movie scene. I want reading what I have to say to be the most interesting option available to the reader in that moment.

Doing this isn't very difficult. It doesn't take a mountain to stop most people in their tracks - a pebble in the road will do. And you can make people read what you write by placing a pebble in the road at the start of your copy.

In copywriting, we call that pebble a 'hook'.

A hook is a short story or anecdote that people find curious or interesting.

A hook might be:

- A short anecdote
- An unusual fact
- A clever quip or saying

They're called hooks because that's literally what they do: hook readers and make them read until the end.

Hooks come in all shapes and sizes. Here's a couple I've used recently:

> John Lennon hated his singing voice. He thought it sounded too thin, so he was constantly screwing around with effects. That's why he sounds so strange on "I Am the Walrus."
>
> You probably do this too when you write... *blah blah blah*

That's a fairly arresting hook. The first two words are a name the reader will recognise. The first sentence is only five words, and it makes a surprising claim that's quickly backed up.

Here's another hook I used recently:

> Las Vegas gambling boss Benny Binion is touring one of his casinos one day, when he finds a group of casino employees huddled around a slot machine combing through swatches of fabric. They're trying to pick a new fabric to cover the stools of the slot machines, and they ask for his opinion.
>
> Binion thinks for a while and replies: "Cover them with butts". It's a great reminder to focus on what counts, and you know it's the same in our industry... *blah blah blah*

A nice, sticky hook I think. The first two words are something most readers will recognise as an exciting concept ('Las Vegas'). The reader is dropped right into the action (Binion touring his casino and making an unusual discovery). The hook closes with a cute pay-off (Binion's reply to his staff), before sending the reader off into our piece.

Using hooks to open your writing is very powerful. I'm surprised more people don't do it. You can seize your reader's attention from the moment you begin.

Try to start everything with a story-driven hook

A student on a course I teach summed up this approach as 'start everything with a story', and she's right: that's basically what this boils down to.

Humans are deeply conditioned to pay attention to stories. It's as though when you tell a story, an ancient bell chimes inside that puts everything else on pause for a few moments. That's the effect you want.

Stories have completely changed the way I write. Before I knew about them, I would always get stuck over how to open a piece. I knew the beginning was important, but I didn't know what I could do to make it compelling.

Stories take care of that for you. You don't need to beg for people's attention. In fact, it's actually difficult for them to stop reading something that you open with a good story.

> **The History of Hooks** In the 19th Century, theatres were rowdy and unruly. Shakespeare knew that when the actors walked out on stage, nobody in the audience would be paying attention. Each performance, a crowd of peasants had to be coaxed away from mead quaffing and turnip hurling (I'm guessing here) to focus on the show.
>
> So, Shakespeare would open his plays with attention-grabbing action-scenes. It's why Hamlet opens with the ghost scene, the Tempest starts with a shipwreck

and Romeo and Juliet begins with Shakespeare basically giving away the ending (the fact that these 'star-crossed lovers' kill themselves) – sacrificing dramatic payoff for a killer opener.

Starting your writing with a story doesn't just gain your audience's attention temporarily, for the duration of that article or blog post. It leaves them more likely to pay attention the *next time* they see your name.

When you start everything you write with a quick, catchy story you earn a reputation for being interesting. In most markets that is rare.

> I publish a weekly newsletter to help you engage people. When I meet my subscribers, they sometimes tell me that they put aside what they're doing when an email from me drops into their inbox. At one bank, they've actually printed off the emails so they can keep them in a binder.
>
> They aren't doing that because of me, they're doing that because of my stories. They've learned that when they get that email from Gatehouse there will be some pleasure, they will derive some value, and it won't be a complete waste of their time.

Let's demystify storytelling

Part of me is reluctant to call this 'storytelling'.

That's because storytelling is often presented in a dry, academic way. It's as though you can't mention storytelling without somebody popping to up explain how stories activate the brain's olfactory and somatosensory cortices, triggering the release of the chemical phenylethanolamine.

Let's get away from that. I love stories because they're simple. You don't need a degree in English Literature to tell a story, or to recognise an attention-grabbing tale. It's human nature.

Storytelling is timeless, too. Fads come and go in business, but storytelling has always worked as a leadership and motivational tool, and always will.

Plus, stories work across all ages and all demographics. You don't have to adapt them to your audience much. And the best ones are contagious. They spread without any extra effort.

They also show a respect for your audience. Stories give people the freedom to come to their own conclusions, and they're a great way to explain what needs to be done without telling them what to do.

Over the next few chapters I'll explain exactly where to find stories, and how to use them to get your message across.

Where to Find Stories to Hook Your Reader

Hopefully you're sold on stories.

Before we continue, let me address something you might be thinking:

> "Ian, I get it – stories make people read stuff. But you know why I don't open everything with a story? I don't have any!"

Well, neither did I. Not until one day, when I decided to start collecting them. Once I realised that people paid more attention to my writing when it opened with a story, I became an anecdote magpie – collecting neat little stories and yarns to make people read my stuff.

 The 'secret of my success' (for want of a better phrase) is that I keep a 'swipe file' of hooks. My swipe file is a collection of stories, anecdotes, and interesting facts that I've collected and saved

My swipe file of stories is my biggest asset as a writer

If I need a story for something I'm writing, I can open it and find one in a few minutes. I never start anything important without scrolling through my swipe file for inspiration. Firstly, let me give you a peep:

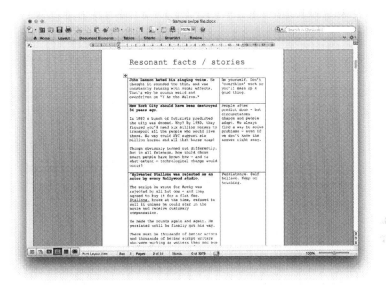

Let me show you some of the things that are in here:

> "When I go to a Mexican restaurant for the first time,
> I always get the enchiladas. If they can't make enchi-
> ladas, they can't make anything else. It's a cornerstone
> of Mexican cooking." *You're My Favourite Client*

I noticed this passage in a book by a graphic designer. It's just a quick story about a simple, amusing test this guy has developed to quickly evaluate a Mexican restaurant.

Maybe I could use this to talk about how important it is to take care of the basics. Maybe I could use it to talk about how you'll never know what your customers will measure on. Maybe I'll never use it at all. It doesn't matter, I don't have to decide now.

Here's another, I found quoted somewhere on Reddit:

> "When reporters asked Shepard what he thought about
> as he sat atop the Redstone rocket, waiting for liftoff,

he had replied, 'The fact that every part of this ship was built by the low bidder.'" *Failure Is Not an Option*

A great little story. Dramatic and insightful. I could open a piece with this if I wanted to communicate:

- Why my thing costs more than my competitor's thing
- How design decisions suddenly matter when you launch
- Why it's important to do things right, because it might be somebody else picking up the pieces

Here's another hook I used recently:

> Mick Jagger's weird, strutting on-stage movements on stage come from the fact that the Rolling Stones used to play very, very small stages. "With our equipment on stage, we'd sometimes have no more room than a table as a viable space to work. The band was two feet behind Mick." *Life, Keith Richards*

I found this in Keith Richards' biography. This stood out because it's an observation about how Mick Jagger's early days defined the rest of his career.

This is a very flexible insight. I can imagine using this to explain how the era in which a company was founded can influence its direction far into the future, or how people's origins are visible when you know what to look for.

When I first started keeping a swipe file I had no real strategy for collecting material. I'd just throw in whatever I stumbled across. Soon though, my swipe file had become so central to how I worked that I realised I needed a more proactive system for adding fresh material to my swipe.

Once a month I put aside time to find fresh stories to add to my collection

Once you start to see the power of building a strong swipe file, you might start doing this too. One thing you'll notice as you start a swipe file is that adding to it becomes a hobby. You'll start reading books just because you think there's a good chance they'll contain some juicy goodies for your library.

 For the rest of this chapter, I'll show you several places to find stories for your swipe file.

Non-fiction books

So, you're on the look out for hooks – stories and anecdotes that you can use to open your copy and grab your reader's attention.

You know one great way to find them? Books. Specifically, non-fiction books. Even more specifically than that, biographies and autobiographies.

Personally, I have a huge book habit. I buy a couple of books a week – solely for the purpose of rooting out great new material that I can use in my writing. As I read them, I keep what I find in my swipe file.

As you find stories, you don't need to know how you'll use them. You might never use some of them. All that matters is that you find material with the potential to hold your audience's attention for a couple of minutes.

Over time, my approach has evolved. When I became serious about collecting stories I'd simply read books I already fancied reading, and just hope that I'd find useful material. But soon I began deliberately targeting books that I thought might be chock-full of stories I could snuffle out for my swipe file – even if I had no underlying interest in reading them.

That's when you know you're hooked on hooks!

Biographies and autobiographies are packed with stories

Books about people tend to feature the kind of anecdotes and stories that you're after. Look for personalities that people admire. Business leaders. Sports stars. Celebrities. Politicians, to some extent.

For example, recently I read Sam Walton's biography:

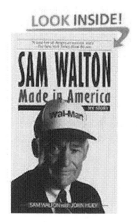

Sam was the founder of Walmart. I chose this book because he's somebody that the audiences I write for will know and admire. Dropping his name at the start of some copy will probably get their attention.

Here's one passage I highlighted:

> If you had to boil down the Wal-Mart system to one single idea, it would probably be communication, because it is one of the real keys to our success. We do it in so many ways, from the Saturday morning meeting to the very simple phone call, to our satellite system. The necessity for good communication in a big company like this is so vital it can't be overstated. What good is figuring out a better way to sell beach towels if you aren't going to tell everybody in your company about it?
> *Sam Walton, Made in America*

Because I spend a lot of time writing about communication, this passage has been pretty useful to me. Sam Walton was the richest person in American for much of the 1980s, so the idea that he valued communication above all else is something that resonates with my audience.

I've boiled this passage down into a quick piece to illustrate the value of communication:

> Walmart founder Sam Walton once said: "What good is figuring out a better way to sell beach towels if you aren't going to tell everybody in your company about it?"

Jack Welch is another business luminary I think my audience admires. I read this book by him to see what stories I could find:

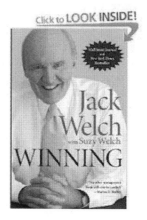

There was plenty of material. For example, here's how Jack describes his goal in communicating his strategy:

> Your direction has to be so vivid that if you randomly woke one of your employees in the middle of the night and asked him, "Where are we going?" he could still answer in a half-asleep stupor: "We're going to keep improving our service to individual contractors and expand our market by aggressively reaching out to small wholesalers. *Winning: The Ultimate Business How-To Book, Jack Welch*

Sometimes you have to look deeper

Sometimes the material isn't handed to you on a plate. Often, it's the the underlying themes that are useful.

A colleague mentioned that one of his heroes is motorbike racing legend Valentino Rossi. I don't know much about motorbikes, but it sounds like an exciting world that might have some parallels with business. So I ordered Rossi's (slightly awkward sounding) autobiography 'What If I Had Never Tried It' to see what I could snag.

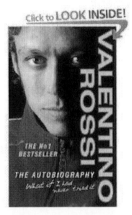

Turned out, a lot. In this book, the anecdotes themselves weren't really that strong – mostly jokes between mechanics in the workshop – but there were some broader take-aways that I found useful.

Valentino Rossi was the Pelé of motorcycle racing. He raced for Honda (the best team) and won the MotoGP (big trophy) five years in a row. But just when he was at the top of his game, he shocked everybody by moving to Yamaha (smaller manufacturer with crappier bikes).

To everybody's amazement he continued his winning streak – scooping even more accolades than before. And the reason he moved from Honda to Yamaha? To prove that it was his skill that won races – not the $9 million Honda superbike underneath him. He wanted to prove it was man over machine.

Oh, boy. I love this story. It has all the makings of a strong hook:

- Motorcycle racing is something people generally recognise as a thrilling activity
- It features several twists (races for Honda, wins everything in sight, shocks fans by leaving, shocks fans again by winning

even more stuff. Reveals reason: to prove winning was him, not bike)

- You can tell this story in 100 words or less

There are good parallels with motivation, leadership, and career here.

There are plenty of possible messages you can draw from it:

- Successful people have to work harder to continue to prove themselves once they've reached the top of their game
- Working for a smaller company provides more opportunity than the market leader

Mark Cuban

Here's another example. One of my colleagues worships the investor Mark Cuban. I checked out his book, and what do you know – lots of stories:

Turns out, when Cuban started his first company (an IT consultancy) he was scared of visiting customers. He was worried that his customers would know more about the industry than he did, and he'd be exposed as an outsider with no experience.

So before every meeting, he'd cram as much as possible on the topics of the day. He'd read every trade magazine going so he could sound knowledgable. In meetings, he'd toss out tidbits here and there - features and bugs he'd read about.

In fact, he was always the best informed person in the room.

> "I expected them to say: "Oh yeah, I read that too in such-and-such." That's not what happened. They hadn't read it then, and they still haven't started reading it. Most people won't put in the time."

A good hook.

It illustrates the reality that once you've read three books on any topic, you're better informed than 99% of people – even those who are fairly established within a field.

I've used this story to make a few different points:

- Often in business you feel out of your depth dealing with different subject matter experts. The truth is, you can probably more than hold your own – often all you really need to do is read a couple of books
- It's fairly easy to 'know enough to be dangerous' in any industry, just by keeping up with the trade magazines

Often, the best anecdotes will be mentioned in passing

The Rolling Stones' Keith Richards mentions this story in his autobiography Life:

> The BBC was giving live coverage to the Beaulieu Jazz Festival in 1961 and they had to actually shut down the broadcast when trad jazz and modern jazz fans started to beat the shit out of each other, and the whole crowd lost control. *Keith Richards, Life*

Can you imagine – jazz fans beefing over two strands of musical genre? I can use this. I highlighted it for my swipe file because I recognised its potential as a nice visual example of how people can get caught up in their passions.

Here's another one that nearly got away, a passage from a novel by Steven Pressfield. This is one of the few items in my swipe file from a work of fiction:

> The Spartans excused the warrior who lost his helmet or breastplate in battle. But they punished with loss of all citizenship rights the man who discards his shield. It was because a warrior carries helmet and breastplate for his own protection, but his shield for the safety of the whole line.

This morsel has a lot going for it: history, warfare, honour and discipline. It's also very flexible – you can deploy this in copy about teamwork or working in organisations.

In the swipe file it goes!

How to Capture What You Read

 I recommend reading on a Kindle, rather than buying a physical book. Here's why: it's much easier to add stuff to your swipe file.

You see, the Kindle has a feature where you can highlight passages. You can then go to the Kindle website and access all your highlights in one place:

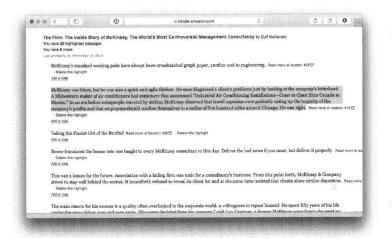

From here, you can copy and paste them into your swipe file. This is the only way to copy and paste material from a Kindle title. If you read the book on your iPhone, iPad, or even through the Kindle web reader you'll find that you can't copy and paste passages.

If you're reading a physical book and you want to save material for your swipe file, you'll just have to highlight passages as you go through with a pen or a fold of the corner, and then return at the end of the book and type everything in. You could also take a photo of the page and run it through an OCR service like http://free-ocr.com if you like.

I know that this sounds like a lot of work, but it makes writing much faster. As Abraham Lincoln said:

"Give me six hours to chop down the tree, and I will spend the first four sharpening the axe."

(Yes, I got that from a book.)

Feeling clever? Target books that seem full of stories

You can get really cute and look for books you know will have some good stories.

For example, there's 116 books in the Amazon Kindle store with the phrase: "most amazing". For example, "The Most Amazing Man Who Ever Lived", "The World's Most Amazing Dog Tales", "Great Gambling Scams: True Stories of the World's Most Amazing Hustles."

I'll wager any of these books is worth checking out for good material to hook an audience.

Rock music is a great world to plunder for hooks

People admire guitar heroes, and re-tell their escapades lets you add excitement to any piece of copy. Plus, telling somebody's story kind of puts a firewall between you and any offence that it may cause.

Rock and roll memoirs are so full of cool anecdotes that I've had to cut back. (I don't want to be typecast as a rock nut!)

Here's some I found in music biographies:

- Ray Davies from The Kinks was told he couldn't sing. His producer's solution was to have him sing "You Really Got Me" in short telegraphic outbursts. You don't have to sing if you're basically saying the words.

- Keith Richards of the Rolling Stones wrote "Satisfaction" in his sleep. He woke up one morning to find it on the cassette recorder he kept by his bed – 3 minutes of strumming followed by 40 minutes of snoring.

Find worlds that intrigue people

Biographies of people your audience finds exciting are a smart way to find anecdotes and stories to hook your audience.

By the same token, books that are effectively biographies of *worlds* that you audience finds exciting are also great to plunder.

Travel is exciting. Here's one passage from Zen and the Art of Motorcycle Maintenance – a father's novel about a summer motorcycle trip taken with his son:

> An untrained observer will often get the idea that physical labor is mainly what the mechanic does. Actually the physical labor is the smallest and easiest part of what the mechanic does. By far the greatest part of his work is careful observation and precise thinking. That is why mechanics sometimes seem so taciturn and withdrawn when performing tests. They don't like it when you talk to them because they are concentrating on mental images, hierarchies, and not really looking at you or the physical motorcycle at all. *Robert Pirsig, Zen and the Art of Motorcycle Maintenance*

I highlighted this passage because I think it resonates with people who sometimes think that other people don't understand their work. (Basically, everybody.)

I've used it several times to good effect. It resonates well with audiences of middle managers, blue collar workers, and senior leaders. Everybody from the shop floor to the corner office identifies with that mechanic working on the Honda: "Nobody gets what I *really* do".

Joining the Mafia

Surely a book about the history of the Sicilian mafia would have a few humdingers to wake up a sleepy audience?

I wasn't disappointed!

Apparently, no one is allowed to introduce himself as a mafioso, even to another man of honour. Instead, they have to go through this elaborate ritual:

> Mafioso 1: God's blood! My tooth hurts! (pointing to one of the upper canines) Mafioso 2: Mine too. Mafioso 1: When did yours hurt? Mafioso 2: On the day of Our Lady of the Annunciation.

LOL, as my great grandmother used to say.

Besides being a faintly comical sketch, I had no idea how I'd use this. I just knew it would be a solid way to open a piece. But I've been able to use this a few times when I've needed to demonstrate something that unites people. I set out what the mafioso do, and then segue with: "In our industry, we don't need this elaborate ritual to recognise each other - one glance at our copy of the Moody's Manual and they know." Hopefully you get the idea.

Stories in space

Space travel is something people find exciting. I read a book about the Apollo 11 mission, and found this story for my swipe file:

> Neil Armstrong had a recurring nightmare in the years running up to the launch of Apollo 11 - the spaceflight that landed the first humans on the moon.
>
> His nightmare was this: he's sat in the lunar module having completed the moon mission, ready to return to earth. He hits the button... but the engines won't start. He's stranded on the moon.
>
> There was some substance to the nightmare. Armstrong knew that the lunar module had no ignition system. Instead, the engine was fired by two hypergolic substances that would ignite on contact. Armstrong wished dearly for a simple mechanical lever that would allow him to physically mix the

fluid. But instead he had to put his faith in a mysterious electrical switch.

During the Apollo 11 mission, Armstrong hit the button - and nothing happened. He was stranded on the moon.

"I started to think of ways to activate the switch" wrote Armstrong later. "As it turned out, the very pen I used to record these notes was the perfect tool to engage this circuit breaker."

This story takes a few paragraphs to tell, but it ticks a lot of boxes.

- It's about somebody well-known that people admire
- It's about something people find exciting (space travel)
- It contains a personal anecdote, a little known fact (the lever), and there's a twist (his nightmare becomes reality)

There are plenty of lessons you could extract from this story:

- It illustrates the idea that your mind often worries about things for a reason.
- It's a reminder to rely on your instinct. Maybe Armstrong should have insisted on that mechanical lever to mix the 'launch juice', rather than trust an unreliable button?

To tell you the truth I've yet to use this story. But every week that goes by you can bet I'm looking for an opportunity.

Kindle Popular Highlights

So, let's recap, in simple caveman speak. Books. Many stories. But reading! Take long time. And expensive. Ug!

If you're lazy, here's a secret: there's actually a way to get Amazon to give you the best parts of any book for free. Not only do you not have to buy the book. You don't even have to *read* it. Yikes! Let me show you how this works.

First of all you want to go to Amazon – but not the homepage – the part of Amazon we're going to be using is http://kindle.amazon.com:

Normally this is the page you come to when you want to look at all the passages you've highlighted on your Amazon Kindle. But that's not why we're here! What we're about to do is look at things that other people have already highlighted for us.

 If you type in a book, Amazon will show you the parts of the book that people reading on their Kindle have highlighted the most times.

And guess what: fortunately for us, the things that people tend to highlight as they read tend to work very well as hooks in our copy.

To get started, search for a book. What I normally do is search for non-fiction books about famous leaders most people admire.

Let's kick off by searching for Nelson Mandela:

The first result is his autobiography. The second result seems to be a kind of anthology of his wisdom. Let's click on the second – that's likely to have more quotable material.

You'll notice that we're not taken to the normal Amazon book page but to a special Kindle highlight page instead. If you scroll down you can see what other people have highlighted.

The first thing you notice is that people love to highlight interesting facts:

"Mandela is indifferent to almost all material possessions – he does not know or care about the names of cars, couches, or

> watches – but I've seen him dispatch a bodyguard to drive an hour to get his favorite pen."

I can imagine bridging out of this into a point about how one thing we're all passionate about is the tools we use. How even the greatest leaders can be left foundering without something small but important. Something like that.

You don't need to know exactly how you're going to use this material now – you just have to be able to spot the potential. So copy and paste that your swipe file and move on.

The next thing that people love to highlight are interesting metaphors. Here's a nice metaphor from Mandela, comparing driving cattle to motivating people:

> "You know, when you want to get the cattle to move in a certain direction, you stand at the back with a stick, and then you get a few of the cleverer cattle to go to the front and move in the direction that you want them to go. The rest of the cattle follow the few more-energetic cattle in the front, but you are really guiding them from the back."

You could definitely use that as a hook if you're trying to articulate your leadership style. Again, paste that into your swipe file and let's continue the hunt.

What we're doing is letting other Amazon readers to do the hard work

Usually, other people have already hunted down the best stories and metaphors. All we have to do is grab them.

Material from legendary figures like Mandela lands really well. He's somebody most people admire, and his quotes, ideas and sayings carry a lot of currency.

Besides world leaders I also like to look at the popular highlights for business authors. Let's search for Chip & Dan Heath for example – they're well respected in business audience. Here you can see that another thing people tend to highlight are interesting findings or statistics.

> In a survey of 10,000 employees from the 1,000 largest companies, 40% of workers cited "lack of recognition" as a key reason for leaving a job.

I write a lot for internal communication audiences, and I'm often looking for examples of people not being satisfied in their roles. A lot of the stuff I sell solves that problem. I find that when I'm scanning for swipe file material, usable material seems to jump out at me.

Sportsmen and women also make great people to search for. My friend Anna Rydne turned me onto this story from a book by Zlatan – the Swedish soccer player:

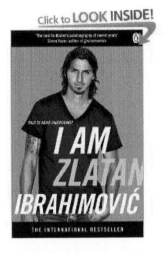

There's one story about him showing some friends around his new apartment, and they criticise his taste in art:

> "I hung a big picture of two dirty feet. When my mates turned up, they were all like, awesome, wicked, cool place you've got here. 'But what are these disgusting feet doing here? How can you have this shit on your wall?' 'You idiots,' I said. 'Those feet have paid for all of this.'"

Those feet have paid for all of this. Beautiful quote. There are so many ways to use that one.

So there you go – Amazon's popular highlights are a little known but amazing way to find the best parts of most books for free. Put aside a few minutes once a week to dig through the popular highlights and see what you can find.

Reddit

As every lazy journalist on deadline knows, Reddit is a 24-hour ATM spitting out wild facts and strange curiosities. Its boards are also a limitless source of fascinating stories you can use in your writing.

Reddit is divided into boards where people discuss different topics. The one we're concerned with is 'TIL', which is Reddit-speak for 'Today I Learned'. People come to http://www.reddit.com/r/todayilearned to post unusual factoids they've discovered:

> TIL that pineapples were such a status symbol in 18th century England that you could rent one for the evening to take to a party

> TIL that when the last woolly mammoths died out, the pyramids of Giza were already a thousand years old

> TIL Pigeons never forget a face. If you chase one away, it will remember you and avoid you in later encounters

Not everything in TIL is great, but if you go to http://reddit.com/r/todayilearned and click the 'top' button in the navigation it will sort the posts by popularity – bringing the cream to the top.

In the spirit of research, let me go to Reddit right now and see what

I can find:

> TIL that we live at the most peaceful time in human history, that violence has been declining both between nations and between people for a millenia, and a person is hundreds of times less likely to die of violence now than 500 years ago. (Source: http://edge.org/conversation/mc2011-history-violence-pinker)

That's interesting. The fact that we're actually living through the most peaceful time in humanity's existence is news to most folk. You could use this to illustrate how we tend to focus on what the media presents us with, rather than studying the big picture.

Quora

> Steve Jobs strolls into the Apple break room one day in 1994 and starts making himself a bagel.
>
> The staff chew warily.
>
> Suddenly, Jobs addresses the room:
>
> "Who is the most powerful person in the world?"
>
> Silence. A few names are proposed. Bill Clinton? Nelson Mandela?
>
> Then, Jobs erupts:
>
> "NO! You are ALL wrong. The most powerful person in the world is the storyteller. The storyteller sets the vision, values and agenda of an entire generation that is to come and Disney has a monopoly on the storyteller business."
>
> He continues:

> "You know what? I am tired of that bullshit, I am going to be the next storyteller"
>
> And out he walks with his bagel

I found this on Quora – another great website for building up your swipe file.

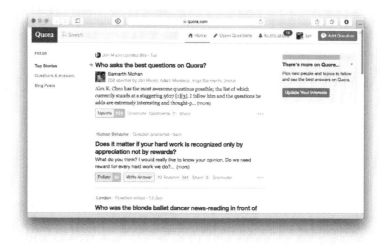

There was a long thread about chance encounters with Steve Jobs, and I saved this story because I think Jobs was right – stories give you power.

Quora is a Q&A website popular in Silicon Valley. It's used by some well-known people, especially in the technology industry. Michael Dell, Stephen Fry, Ashton Kutcher all pop-up.

On Quora, people post questions ("What happened to Marina Oswald, Lee Harvey Oswald's widow?") and others weigh in with answers. There are several other Q&A websites, but Quora is unusual because the quality of the writing is very high. People put a lot of care into their answers. Confusing copy isn't tolerated by the community.

Most of the questions are looking for background on a specific topic:

- How often should jeans be washed?
- How long does an eagle egg take to hatch?

But Quora also has some more open-ended questions that throw up a treasure-trove of useful nuggets. For example, there's thread called: "What are some of the most interesting little-known things?"

Somebody has replied with a picture of where the Baltic sea meets the north sea. It's amazing - the water doesn't mix:

Another thread titled "What are some mind-blowing facts about the human body?" has the fact that humans share 50% of our DNA with bananas. Another fact I found on Quora (but can't remember where) is that Facebook is blue because Mark Zuckerberg has red/green colour blindness.

Once again you don't need to know how this material will be useful. If it's interesting, keep it in your swipe file. There's a good chance it will come in useful – either to grab a reader's attention or to hold on to it.

Listening and Tuning In

The copywriter Eugene Schwartz once said: "You don't have to have great ideas if you can hear great ideas."

I wrote one of my best performing pieces just by listening to a story told to me by an amateur pilot. I used it in an email almost word for word – all I did was stick a call to action on the end.

I could tell you the story, but I might as well just show you the email I got out of it:

> My friend Bob Etherington flies planes. He told me what happens when you're coming in to land: First, you hear your co-pilot counting down the approach:
>
> - "8 miles, 10,000 feet."
> - "6 miles, 6,000 feet."
> - "4 miles, 2,000 feet."
>
> Finally, he says:
>
> "2 miles to run, 1,000 feet - DECIDE."
>
> At this point, the only responses the pilot can give are "LAND" or "GO AROUND" (not "Oo-er, I'm not sure - what do you think?")
>
> You have to DECIDE.
>
> Today is your day to decide for Accelerate - the 4 day intensive development program that we're delivering with the Institute of Internal Communication.

We have one place left - and you only have until the end of today (Wednesday 17th October 2012) to book. See if it's for you and DECIDE.

Thanks

Ian

I had a great response to this. One lady even emailed me back with this:

Hello Ian

I'm not going on the course, but I must say that's the best written marketing email I've received in living memory!

Victoria

And all because I kept my ears open.

When you tune in, stories appear

The weird thing is that once you start collecting stories, the world seems to do its best to bring them to you. It's like the universe conspires to help you. I know this sounds weird. We're getting into The Secret territory here - the law of attraction, and all that stuff. Stephen Pressfield says it's to do with angels. I'm not going that far thanks, but whatever it is it works.

Seek and ye shall find.

I think that's from a book, too.

How to Link a Story to Your Message

Stories are brilliant for capturing people's attention. I'm amazed that more people don't use them, because as you've seen it's not hard to find good stories that will hook your audience and keep them coming back for more.

But grabbing people's attention is one thing: once you have their attention, you need to deliver your message.

 The way to link your story to the thing you ultimately want to communicate) is to use a simple writing trick called a bridge

A bridge is a simple technique that lets you seamlessly transition from your hook into your message without losing your reader's attention.

Knowing how to bridge is very important if you're serious about using stories in your writing. Unless you build up to a solid point, your reader's interest will eventually fizzle away. Stories are lovely, but without a way to make them relevant to your audience people will begin to tune out.

It's when you combine a killer story with a relevant message – when you mix the sugar with the medicine – that you become somebody worth following.

I came up with the concept of bridging because I knew I needed to find a way to blend the story with my message:

> "Okay, here's a lovely story about a band of Japanese soldiers who carried on fighting World War II until the

1970s because they refused to believe they'd lost. How can I how can I tell this in a way that's relevant to my audience of management consultants?"

There's always a way, and it's usually much simpler than you think.

14 sample bridges

- I love this story because it shows...
- It's a nice reminder of how...
- It's the same in our industry
- Clearly, there's an important lesson here for us
- What's the takeaway here?
- Why am I sharing this?
- What am I saying?
- What this all boils down to is...
- Here's the point:
- What I'm saying is this:
- Bottom-line:
- One last thought:
- Now I'd like to emphasise something here:
- Hearing this story makes me think of...

Let me show you some examples:

Why am I sharing this? Often in organisations like ours, it's easy to forget how our role aligns with the firm's overall strategy.

Here's the point: we're all responsible for our company's brand.

Now I'd like to emphasise something here: the soldiers didn't succeed because they followed the map down from the mountain, but because they took action.

With practice you can seamlessly segue from any story into the actual point you want to make. Usually, all you have to say is: "I love this story because..." and then talk about what the story you just shared has to do with your audience.

Where to put your bridge

The bridge can come anywhere in your copy – there's no rule to say where you have to put it. It can come at the beginning, or right at the end.

 If you know your audience well and you have a strong story to tell, you can leave your message until the end. But if you're writing to a cold audience – people who aren't familiar with your work – you should bridge sooner rather than later. Cold audiences will still enjoy the story, but if you don't get to the point soon they might think you aren't going to take them anywhere relevant.

In the example below, the bridge comes right at the end of a 300 word story. I can only do that because the audience I'm writing to is 'warm': in other words they're used to hearing from me. They know that I always open with a strong story, and they know that I always get to a relevant point in the end:

> David Lee Roth jumps down from the Van Halen tour bus and makes a bee-line for the concert hall. He strides into the dressing room and immediately locates the object he's looking for – a little bowl of peanut M&M's.
>
> Roth begins to sort through the sweets, carefully inspecting each one. If he finds a single brown M&M, tonight's show could be off.
>
> Van Halen's tour rider explicitly specified:
>
> "M&M's (WARNING: ABSOLUTELY NO BROWN ONES)."
>
> This story has been part of rock folklore for years. But the truth recently came to light – and it's a great lesson in communication.
>
> Turns out Roth's behaviour wasn't unreasonable at all. To understand why he was so adamant about the M&M's clause, you first have to realise that Van Halen's '1984 Tour' was the biggest, most complex show in rock history.
>
> "Van Halen was the first to take 850 par lamp lights — huge lights — around the country," says David Lee Roth. "At the time, it was the biggest production ever."
>
> Venues had to pay careful attention to the band's elaborate instructions explaining how to rig the venue for the show.
>
> Most didn't bother, and the band would roll up with nine 18-wheel trucks only to find the show couldn't go ahead because venue hadn't done the right groundwork.
>
> So Roth's M&M's test was a quick way to see who'd read the show's technical specifications and who hadn't.
>
> "If I came backstage and I saw brown M&M's on the catering table, it guaranteed the promoter had not read the contract

rider, and we had to do a serious line check," says Roth.

I love this story because as a professional communicator you probably accept that not everybody reads the important material you give them.

The question is – is there an M&M's test you can apply to your own material so you always know when you're ready to rock?

As I said, the bridge came right at the end. I was confident that story was strong enough to hold their attention right the way through.

To be honest the bridge was pretty weak. "Is there an M&M's test you can apply to your own material?" I'm not even sure what that means, now I think of it! But this blog post was one of the most popular I'd ever ran. It went wild with people sharing it via email.

None of it was down to me – the story did all the work. And the bridge made it *just* relevant enough for them to feel comfortable sharing it with friends in their industry.

Here's another. This time, the bridge is in the middle. In an ideal world, I'd use this with an audience I don't know so well. In other words, an audience that I want to hook them with a strong story, but I don't want to keep waiting before I deliver value:

You're tricked each time you book a flight or hotel room.

When the site says it's searching, it's often keeping you waiting artificially. Why? It knows that if it displays your results too quickly you'll think it didn't look properly.

It's the 'locksmith effect'.

A locksmith can open your door in seconds, but he still goes through a theatrical production to make you feel as though you got your money's worth.

It's like that in our industry.

A senior manager asks for your opinion. You fire back the answer. They go ahead and ignore you. Why? The locksmith effect.

Most people only value work they believe the other side has paid for with their sweat. So next time somebody needs your help, take a deep breath - quite often the longer you take to respond the more likely they'll be to buy your answer.

Notice how the bridge ("It's like that in our industry") lets me pivot right into the meat? It just takes one line. That's the beauty of the bridge!

Don't overdo your bridge!

I love bridges because they let you make a clean break – deftly escaping your story and pivoting into your message.

 I used to get this completely wrong. I would really 'go to town' on my bridge – taking great pains to ram home exactly why the story I'd just shared was relevant. So if I spent 300 words developing my hook, I'd spend another 300 words on the bridge – tying it all together and making a watertight comparison.

What happens is that I sounded like a preacher delivering a sermon. I'd keep yo-yoing back to the hook again and again, making sure everybody understood the connection.

Don't overdo it. I know it might feels like you need a solid 'excuse' for sharing the story that you've just told them, but honestly – if a story's good enough, nobody really cares why you shared it with them. They're just grateful you did.

Look at it this way: ultimately, you and your reader are co-conspirators: they want the candy, you want the attention.

Is your story more important than your message?

I'll let you into a secret.

A lot of the time when I sit down to write something, I pick the story that I'll use as my hook before I even know what I'm writing about. I work 'back to front'.

You'll find the best stories will burn a hole in your pocket. So, you naturally look for ways to share them with your audience.

I actually find working this way much faster, because once I've got a catchy story the rest usually writes itself. So I was pleased to discover that songwriting works the same way.

 Apparently, Paul McCartney came up with the melody to Yesterday in his sleep – and wrote the lyrics by just shouting words into the mic. (The placeholder words he used were 'Scrambled eggs'.)

You hear this time and time again in music memoirs: the lyrics to legendary songs were almost an afterthought. The artist created the melody first - the overall feel of the song - and filled in the content (the lyrics) later. I'd always thought it was the other way round, that the music had to fit around the words. Apparently not.

There's a nice writing lesson here. A lot of people think that when you write, you should first decide what you want to say – get your message as tight as possible – and then come up with some funky way to say it.

That's sensible enough. But increasingly, I'll do it the other way round:

I'll dig up a great story, and then I'll look around for a message I can attach to it

I think this approach makes sense a lot of the time. A month or a year from now, most of your audience won't remember the message you're delivering - but they *will* fondly recall the story you told. Remember, if you tell stories that people enjoy, your audience will soon come to recognise you as somebody worth paying attention to. ("Wonder what she's got for me today?")

11 Writing Hacks

We've spent a lot of time talking about getting people to read what you write. And to be honest, that is most of the battle. But what about once you have their attention? How do you keep them reading?

To be honest, it's mostly about saying what you have to say as simply and as clearly as possible. It can seem more complicated, but only because many writers want to make it that way.

> Good writing is invisible to the reader – he should not be aware he's reading something. Instead, your copy should smoothly melt into the conversation already going on in his head. *Dan Kennedy*

Here's some advice that's helped me:

Only communicate one idea

Former British Prime Minister Harold MacMillan supposedly once gave a young Member of Parliament some advice on a speech:

> "When you've been an MP for between one and ten years your speech should contain no more than one point. When you've been an MP for between ten and twenty years you'll have enough experience to raise it to two points. Anything over

> twenty years as an MP and you can raise it to three points but
> that's it! Three points, maximum, is all you'll get across in any
> speech!"

There's so much truth in that. When you're writing, make one point
and make it well.

Keep your writing lean

Good writing is about removing words, not adding them.

One day Oscar Wilde wondered how his new book was selling. So
he telegraphed his London publisher a single character: "?"

The publisher cabled back: "!"

Most of us agree that in communication, shorter is generally better.
The problem is, a lot of us enjoy writing. (Especially you, reading a
book about it.) It's that passion that sometimes makes our writing
longer than it needs to be.

I've always thought it strange that many writers will half-jokingly
use food metaphors to talk about their work: people's LinkedIn
bios describe them 'serving up sizzling copy', and writing 'delicious
copy' that leaves you 'hungry for more'.

You hear amateur copywriters talking about themselves as 'word-
smiths'. It's not the addition of words. It's the subtraction. Your
writing shouldn't sparkle. It shouldn't dazzle, or glisten or gleam. It
shouldn't sizzle, scintillate or surprise. It shouldn't be sumptuous,
scrumptious or 'finger-licking good'.

Being a good writer is actually about removing as many words as
possible. Style isn't something you *add*, layered on like a sauce. It's
the *absence* of unnecessary ideas.

Leave out the boring parts

Take a tip from Elmore Leonard: leave out the parts that people skip.

Your biggest challenge when you have write isn't knowing what to put in - it's knowing what to leave out.

You lose people if you leave in too much information they don't care about. And you also lose people if you cut content that should stay - information they *want* to read about. Tricky. So what you can do is find somebody from your readership (preferably several people) and ask them to read your email or newsletter before anybody else.

But – and this is important – you tell them not to read the whole piece. Just read to the point where they're are no longer interested in what you're saying.

> You don't want to know what they "think" of the copy. You don't want to know if they found any spelling mistakes or grammar errors. All you want to know is where they got bored or lost interest.

And every time they tell you where they got bored (especially if multiple people are telling me the same thing) you completely eliminate that part of the copy. Then you find somebody else, and somebody else, and keep asking people to read it until they're bored.

This takes time. It's not practical to do this for everything you write. But when you desperately need to hit a home run it's a fool-proof way to edit out anything not absolutely fascinating to your reader.

Go back and try to do what novelist Elmore Leonard said: "Just leave out the boring bits."

One great way to run this test is by grabbing people who are on their way to the toilet. "Hey, can you read this really quickly?" Since they need to pee, they'll give you some straight feedback without fooling around.

Put your neck on the line

The durian fruit is wildly popular in SouthEast Asia. It has a distinctive odour – either stale baby sick or raw sewage, depending on who you ask.

Its smell is so offensive that in Thailand it's banned from government buildings. There are YouTube videos of people cutting one open and throwing up.

But across South East Asia it's considered a delicacy – revered as the king of fruits! Get past the smell and it tastes soft and creamy, like custard mixed with almonds.

So a few years ago, a Thai government scientist had a brainwave – what if you could cross-breed a durian that tasted the same but had no smell? Wouldn't that be a hit?

In 2007 he did it. After decades of research, he finally created an odourless durian.

The fruit was a flop. People who hated durian didn't care about the new odourless variety. And people who loved durian just missed the smell.

In business, many of us communicate like the neutered durian. We write in a so-so corporate style that's easy to ignore. What we write goes in one ear and out the other — presuming it gets read at all. Like the cross-bred durian, we become irrelevant.

What the Thai government scientist should have done is created a durian that stank even more. When you're writing, stick your neck out and create a stink.

> Corporate writing and academic writing 'hedges'. It presents one point of view, and counters with another point of view. Which is right? Most of the time, "it remains to be seen." Don't put your reader through that. Stand for something. Like the writer John Vorhaus says: "Keep your heart where everyone can see it."

Never make the reader wait until the end to find out what to think or do.

- First, summarise your argument
- Then, argue it
- Finally, tell them what to do

You want to be like the Scottish vicar who explained his sermons thus:

> "First, I tell 'em what I'm gonna tell 'em. Then, I tell 'em. Then, I tell 'em what I told 'em."

Add 'whimsy' to your writing

Have you noticed the playful, friendly writing style that consumer brands use now?

It has a name: 'whimsy'.

When you read "Shake it up baby!" in the small print on a smoothie bottle, that's whimsy. When you read "Made in the UK. After all, it's nice here!" on a shampoo bottle, that's whimsy.

Whimsy is a dollop of cute. It's how you're supposed to write now to connect with Generation Y – people under 30.

This perhaps isn't a trendy thing to say, but whimsy can feel a bit 'yuck'. For example, here's a job advert for Innocent drinks:

> *"The role will require you to use lots of lovely category and shopper data to deliver category focused plans that will help maximise the potential sales growth in the chilled juice category, through delivering objective, insight driven advice and recommendations."*

The whimsy ("...lots of lovely category and shopper data...") is snuffed out by the corp-speak that follows.

So, how do you get whimsy right? The easiest way to add whimsy is to plug unexpected human reactions or outbursts into otherwise ordinary sentences.

Look at this line in a post by Gawker writer Caity Weaver:

> Despite refusing to authenticate the painting two decades earlier, museum officials asked to re-examine the work in 2011. This time when they looked at it, they realised, whoopsie, it's real.

Another good way to add whimsy is to summarise a complicated idea in five words. For extra whimsy, have this line immediately follow a longer and more complex sentence.

Here's a good example. It's a letter that Warren Buffett sent to Berkshire Hathaway Inc shareholders in 1984:

> *In line with this owner-orientation, our directors are all major
> shareholders of Berkshire Hathaway. In the case of at least
> four of the five, over 50% of family net worth is represented by
> holdings of Berkshire. We eat our own cooking.*

The whimsy in that paragraph ("We eat our own cooking") adds
a little flash of personality. A knowing wink. A signal that while
Buffett's taking this stuff seriously, he recognises it's not life and
death.

Here's another:

> *With Heinz, Berkshire now owns 8 1/2 companies that, were
> they stand-alone businesses, would be in the Fortune 500. Only
> 491 1/2 to go.*

You need to be careful with whimsy. You're trying to communicate
confidence, not childishness.

For example, Warren Buffett can get away with quoting Woody
Allen like this in an annual report because he's Warren Buffett. I
wouldn't exactly dare you to try it:

> *Our flexibility in capital allocation – our willingness to invest
> large sums passively in non-controlled businesses – gives us a
> significant advantage over companies that limit themselves to
> acquisitions they can operate. Woody Allen stated the general
> idea when he said: "The advantage of being bi-sexual is that
> it doubles your chances for a date on Saturday night." Simi-
> larly, our appetite for either operating businesses or passive
> investments doubles our chances of finding sensible uses for*

our endless gusher of cash.

You're only ever writing for one person

From 1960 to 1964, the Beatles experienced a blast-off success. Sell-out shows. Hysterical fans. Beatlemania. As it happens, copywriting was one secret behind their rapid explosion.

Early Beatles hits were deliberately written in the first person to ensure that lyrics resonated with teenage girls.

When the Fab Four sung "I Want to Hold Your Hand", it was designed to trigger that weak-kneed hysteria you've seen in old news footage.

Songs like "Baby It's You", "From Me to You", and "I Wanna Be Your Man" relentlessly exploited the power of the first person, and turned major stadium events into intimate and highly emotional experiences.

Always write for a person, not a crowd. Because as Lennon and McCartney demonstrated nearly 50 years ago, however big your audience is, you're only ever playing to one person.

Favour 'you' over 'me'

Truffle oil is considered 'cheating' by experienced chefs, because a quick drizzle makes most food taste amazing.

Copywriters have a similar cheat: the 'you/me' ratio.

Do you ever notice how some words leap straight off the page? One of the most powerful words in the English language is 'You'. If you ever need a magnetic word to start a sentence, pick "You".

In fact, if you're enjoying this book, it might be because it has a you/me ratio of 7:1. In other words, I've talked about you 7 times more than I've talked about me. Is this why you're still reading? Could be.

Get to the point

My English teacher used to insist that essays needed a rambling introduction and a lengthy conclusion. If I had anything to say, it had to be squashed into the middle.

This taught you that it's okay to hold off on 'getting to the point'. That's why so many business document and emails take forever to warm up.

Today, you don't have the luxury of carefully setting the scene, or creating a warm, fuzzy preamble. We're busy! Jump in and make your point. Get in, get out.

Use short words

At school, using big words got you better marks. Nothing wrong with that – trotting out six syllable tongue-twisters helped to increase your vocabulary. But it also taught you to garnish your writing with pretentious words and corporate jargon.

Nobody's stood over your desk handing out house points for being Wordsworth anymore. In business, your goal is to be clear and persuasive – not score points for swallowing a thesaurus.

Write actively

The ultimate English teacher no-no? Directly referring to yourself or to your reader.

"*The liquid in the test tube was heated to 80 degrees*" was ok, but the active form ("*I heated the liquid in the test tube to 80 degrees*") wasn't.

Your school taught you that using the passive form made you sound formal and objective.

Time to wise up, because today the opposite is true in business writing. When you address people as "you", they're more likely to tune into your words. And when you refer to yourself as "I", it makes you sound accountable.

Remember, you never have a captive audience

Did you notice how, when you handed in your homework, it always came back marked? That's because your teachers cared deeply about your progress.

You learned that everything you wrote would be carefully read by a trained professional.

The reality could not be more different.

5 Ways to Write Faster

How to Write, Even When You Don't Want To

Clyde Beatty was the world's first celebrity lion tamer.

He climbed into cages filled with lions, tigers, cougars and hyenas, delighting crowds in the 1930s. As he danced left and right, the audience thought it was his whip and his pistol that kept the beasts at bay. In fact, it was the chair.

What Beatty discovered was that when you hold a chair towards a snarling lion, it tries to focus on all four legs at once. Overloaded with options, the animal chooses to freeze instead of fight. (Usually, anyway.)

When you write, you're like the lion faced with the chair. You focus on too much so you don't get anything done. It's called writer's block.

Writer's block is such a common complaint it's become a creative cliché. (The blank page blues!) And it's true: making yourself sit down to write is actually harder than writing itself.

You'll find a thousand helpful articles on 'beating writer's block'.

One tells you to talk to an imaginary friend. Another suggests getting up and washing the dishes. Another tells you to launch Microsoft Word, open a blank document and type: "I am a writer, writers write" over and over again.

Hmm.

Here, I'll share five things that work for me:

1. Stalk the desk

I once heard an interview with copywriter John Carlton (known as the copywriter's copywriter) where he explained a technique called 'stalking the desk'.

Stalking the desk is based on a simple theory – when you're sat at your computer and nothing's coming out, you're not ready to start writing. Get away from that screen, Hemingway.

Stalking the desk is why, whenever I have something difficult to write, I'm never in my seat.

I'll be making coffee. Gazing out of the window. Bugging everyone else. To the rest of the world, it looks like I'm slacking off. But I'm not, I'm 'stalking the desk'.

Stalking the desk means pacing around. Scratching your head. Chewing it over. Basically, doing anything except sitting at your computer.

The minute it comes to you (and it will), dive straight back to your seat and get it all down.

Only sit at your computer when the words are starting to burn their way out.

In fact when I think back, the best writing I've produced was some of the easiest to write. It seemed to spring from some well of divine inspiration. What's more, I don't think I've written anything great that felt like pulling teeth.

Next time you think you have writer's block, ask yourself if you're really 'blocked' or if you're actually empty. If so, get up out of your chair!

2. Start anywhere

Here's something else that makes it easier to get started – there's no law that says you have to write in the correct order. Just dive in – anywhere!

I used to be a staff writer on a computer magazine. I'd have to write reviews of computer monitors, printers and games. I'd waste hours watching the cursor blink, wondering how to start a review in the wittiest way possible. Somewhere along the way, I realised things came together a lot faster if I wrote the straight facts first – the meat of my review – and then just top and tail it with a clever intro or outro.

You can do the same thing whatever you're writing.

When you're preparing to write something, you normally have at least some idea of what part of it will look like. So write that bit first, and damn the rest!

You can imagine how you'll reassure the investor that next quarter's results will look better once the exceptional restructuring costs are out of the way. So write that bit.

If you're writing a press release for the new Harley dealership in Lake Tahoe, you know the details - it's off I-95, it has a parts centre and workshop - even if you don't know how you'll start or finish the rest. So write that bit.

You know the name of the General Manager you hired and what their role is, so get that down even if you don't know how or why or whether to explain why her predecessor was fired.

So write that bit. You get the idea - just write the bit that you can. Usually, more will follow.

3. Write with the door closed, edit with the door open

Now the thing you'll notice, as you bravely 'get started', is that most of what you write won't be very good. That's fine. It's actually normal.

Try to write so fast that you outrun your own doubt.

If there's a 'big secret' to writing, it's that you don't have to get it right first time. Are you using a typewriter? No! (Unless you're Tom Hanks – who has a fetish for vintage Smith Corona Skyriters.) So you have the luxury of going back and editing your work.

LinkedIn 'influencers'. Celebrity bloggers. New York Times columnists. Do you think their writing flows from their fingers ready for print? It doesn't. It clatters out in dribs and drabs. Some of it good, most of it meh.

What a lot of people do is peck out a few words, read them back, change the beginning, futz with the middle and then delete the lot and start again. A couple more times and they give up.

Now this is a piece of advice I'm not always able to stick to. Right now there's something in the previous sentence that sticks out a bit. I want to go back and change it. Maybe I will maybe I won't but for now I'll resist the temptation and carry on because the important part is writing. Editing comes later.

Stephen King's book On Writing is the definitive work on the productivity of writing. He says: "Write with the door closed, rewrite with the door open." What he means is that you just need to get it down on the page without worrying whether it's any good.

The first draft is where you explain it to yourself. The second draft is where you try to explain it to your reader. In other words, when you write your first draft – don't worry about getting it right. Don't worry about it even making sense. The door is closed. Nobody will see it, so stop worrying and nit-picking as you go along.

When you come back and edit, that's when you get to worry about how it reads. The door is open.

King releases a book every year.

Authors envy his work ethic. Whatever you think of his novels, he's doing something right.

For a long time I wouldn't write a first draft at all – I'd try to write the whole thing in one go, like somebody weaving a Persian rug. What would happen is that I'd tie myself in knots editing as I went along.

That's probably the worst thing you can do productivity-wise.

Next time you write, try to have the attitude of: "I'm going to fix everything later."

Was that the best choice of word? Doesn't matter, move on. Could I make that clearer? Doesn't matter, move on.

Your objective is to write fast enough so that doubt can't catch up with you.

Think Newton's First Law: objects in motion tend to stay in motion.

4. Write wherever you can

If you ever pick up a creative writing magazine (tip: don't) you'll see adverts for writer's retreats.

It's where you pay to go to a writer's colony – set in idyllic woods – where you spend the day scribbling away in your own little cabin.

Every lunchtime, a waiter arrives with a little lunchbox – and quietly sets it down outside so as not to disturb the creative process.

There's a certain voice inside us all that wants to postpone writing until it's quiet. Until the environment is perfect. Until the stars align.

It's the mark of a wannabe. Pros write anywhere and everywhere.

> On my kids' life this is true. I'm writing this sentence crouched in the corner of my 11 month old twins' bedroom. Imogen, the eldest by 22 minutes has just gone to sleep, and I'm filling the six or seven minutes until I can safely tiptoe out the door writing on my iPhone's built in Notes app, shielding the screen's glow from the cot.
>
> You can – and should – write anywhere. Drop the idea that you need the perfect creative environment.
>
> True, most of what you create on the go won't be very good. It will be jumbled up, in a random order. It doesn't matter. You'll have something.
>
> For instance, take what I'm writing now for example. I have no idea where this part will go in the book. What happened was, 20 minutes ago, as I was waltzing a baby to sleep - I had the idea that I should cover the concept of writing in snitches and snatches in the book.
>
> So here I am, getting it down.

I do this every day. I spend 90 minutes a day on the bus, and half of that I spend writing. I just open up my phone and start typing. Later when I'm at my computer I can copy the text and rearrange the parts however I like.

Some of it will be rubbish – I'll delete that. Some of it will be okay. I'll keep that. The important part is, I'm writing.

Why is getting started so important? It's important because kicking off, getting going, creates magic. I don't know why, but when you're writing the world helps.

Heaven comes to your aid. The universe gets behind your cause. Ideas appear. Eureka. ### 5. Just get started

You walk into a room and find a small white box.

Carefully, you open the lid. What do you see inside?

Some people say a diamond. Some people say an apple. Some people say a frog. It doesn't really matter. The point is, the box is never empty.

I heard this from somebody who trains comedians to do improv. Her students are terrified that when they stand up in front of an audience, they'll draw a total blank. But what she teaches them – using exercises like this – is that you always come up with something.

Start writing. The box is never empty.

10 Ways to Make Your Writing Look Easy to Read

Go to a bookshelf and pick up a book. I bet you can tell straight away whether it's easy to read. You want people to take one look at your work and *know* it's going to be a pleasure to consume.

Jakob Nielson published a web usability that found 79% of web users scan rather than read. Oh, and this was back in 1997. Do you think, in all the years since that study took place, that people pay more attention or less attention to writing?

Today, it's more important than ever to make your writing look inviting.

People scan what you write to try and get the gist. Only once they're *sure* you're not wasting their time will they settle in and read properly. Here are some ways I try to make my writing look like it's worth reading:

1. Put the first sentence on a line all by itself

Make your first sentence as short as possible, and put it on its own line.

The standalone opener gives a little signal to the reader that what they're about to read is *simple*:

> I'm in a bad situation at work.

> I wanted to make money so I moved to New York.

> Berkshire's gain in net worth during 2013 was $34.2 billion.

2. Keep your column widths tight

Great writers have a secret weapon: short column widths. Readers find it much easier to read something when their eye doesn't have to make several 'saccades' back and forth across the text. Nobody realises this, of course. But short column widths definitely make your writing more likely to be read.

If you're working in Word, drag the margin in. If you're sending an email, hit return every 60 characters.

3. Keep your sentences short

Favour short sentences over long sentences.

4. Put a line break after every idea

The 'wall of text' is one of the biggest turn-offs around. When you land on a piece of writing and you see there's more text than white space it's an immediate signal that there's a hard slog ahead.

The easiest way to stop this happening is to put plenty of line breaks in your writing. Try to have one idea per paragraph. This way you'll naturally end up putting a line break every four or five sentences.

5. Put bullets where they can see them

Bullet points make any piece of text look inviting. They're a signal that the copy is going to be easy to read. Make sure your writing has bullet points 'above the fold', so that as soon as your reader sees the writing the bullet points are visible. In design, they're known as a 'point of entry' because they draw the eye in. Take care to write your bullet points as clearly as possible, because bullets are often the first thing that your reader reads.

6. Open with a quote

"The thing about quotes on the internet is that you cannot confirm their validity." *Abraham Lincoln*

This trick isn't one for every piece, but lazy eyeballs love copy that starts with a quote. Quotation marks indicate speech, and to the brain speech is easy to read.

You can open with a famous quote from a relevant figure, or you can use somebody you've quoted in your piece.

7. Include a picture of a person

I used to think that adding pictures to my copy was kind of cheating. But there's a reason magazine covers feature people's faces. Your eye is drawn to another pair of eyes.

At the least, you can probably have a photograph of yourself.

8. Caption every picture

If you do include pictures, always write captions. Research shows that when people assess a page, picture captions are one of the first things they'll scan when deciding if it's worth their attention.

9. Sign your work

I often put my little signature at the bottom of things I write:

Besides adding a touch of whimsy, it's a visual signal of where the end of my piece is. When you glance at the copy, I want you to know that it won't take you long to read.

10. P.S...

Have you ever wondered why a lot of marketing emails use a postscript (a P.S.)? I used to think it looked amateurish. The reason is that – just like captions – the P.S. is one page element that people read first.

Now, I use a P.S. if the format is appropriate – for example, if I'm writing an email. The trick I use is to basically sum up the entire message in the P.S. That way, even if somebody *only* reads the postscript, they've still got my message.

How to Measure Your Writing

Writing is seen as an art. Something subjective that you feel, but can't really measure. Turns out, that's not true.

In Tim Ferriss's book The 4 Hour Body, he features the case study of Phil Libin. Phil wanted to lose weight, but he'd failed at both dieting and exercise on and off for years. Finally, he decided to see what effect doing nothing would have.

Each morning before breakfast he weighed himself naked and plotted the result on a chart, but apart from that he made no conscious effort to change his habits. He lost two stone (12Kg) in six months.

He found that just by monitoring that one statistic – his weight – he could effect change.

In writing, you also have a statistic you can monitor that tells you how well you're doing

It's called the Flesch Reading Ease test – otherwise known as the 'readability score'.

The FK score tells you how easy your writing is to read. It gives it a score based on how long the words you choose are and how many syllables they contain. It's a very reliable indicator of how easy your writing is to read.

You can run your copy through it to find out how easy it is to read on a scale of 0 to 100. The higher the score, the easier it is to read. It's not perfect, but it's pretty accurate.

For example, read this:

> Advocates for military intervention in Syria this summer invariably pointed to a prevailing international norm when making their case. Military action, they argued, was the only way to enforce the worldwide prohibition against the use of chemical weapons.

This passage has a reading ease score of 29.5 out of 100. That's low. You need to be about 21 to easily understand it.

Contrast that with the book you're reading now, which has a reading ease score of 74.1. It should be easily understood by 12 to 13 year olds.

Some copywriters sneer at this tool, but the kind of writers that I admire love it.

> Copywriter John Fancher talks about texting colleagues:
>
> "85!" "90!" "92!"

His friends know what he means just by the numbers. It means he's written something that's so simple a kid could read it.

And yes, he's proud of this. You should be too. Why? Because simple words communicate. If you can take a complex idea and communicate it simply, that's a very valuable skill.

There are other writing tools – Gunning Fog, the SMOG Index, the Coleman Liau Index. I wouldn't worry too much about the differences. Most of the time they tell you the same thing.

I check my reading scores all the time. It's a great way to get an idea of how well your message is coming across. It's not perfect, but if you run your copy through it and you get back "30 out of 100" it's a red flag to revise.

Storytelling kit

A collection of flexible stories you can use to lead and inspire

Marvin Bower, the founder of the modern-day McKinsey & Company, put his success down to a quality that most people overlook: a willingness to repeat himself.

Bower spent fifty years of his life saying the same thing over and over again. He never deviated from his message as he established the culture and practices that made McKinsey so successful.

Being a great leader is about repetition and consistency. It's about finding new ways to say the same thing, day after day, year after year.

The best way to do that is to use stories.

I've shown you plenty of pages to find stories, but to give you a kick-start, here's some that I've collected that you can use yourself.

I hope you find them useful.

How to use this storytelling kit

These stories will help you deliver your message in a way that people will enjoy listening to.

I've given you 12 stories and 14 bridges.

- Each **story** is designed to be short and powerful, and flexible enough for you to attach a range of different leadership messages

- Each **bridge** is a short sentence that will allow you to switch from your story into your message without losing your audience

What you do is pick a story you think will capture your audience's attention, and then use one of the bridges to mix neatly into the thing you actually want to say.

Alongside each story I've provided some suggestions for how you might use it.

Remember, humans are deeply conditioned to pay attention to stories. I hope by giving you these stories, you will be able to start using them to lead.

If you need any help, don't be afraid to get in touch.

Ian ☺

Ian Harris
Associate Director, Gatehouse
i.harris@gatehousegroup.co.uk
http://www.gatehouse.co.uk

Story 1: NASA

During the 1960s space race, NASA hit a problem.

Astronauts couldn't write in space, because ordinary pens wouldn't work in zero gravity.

So according to legend, NASA hired Paul Fisher to design a pen that would write in space. Months later, after $1.5 million of research, he came up with a solution.

At last, NASA had a state-of-the-art pen that:

- Worked in zero gravity
- Performed in a vacuum
- Could cope with a drastic temperature range

Of course, the Russian cosmonauts had the same problem. So they used a pencil.

I love this story because it shows how smart people often waste time creating elaborate solutions to problems when a simple answer is right under their nose.

> **How to use this story**
> People over-engineer solutions to things in most industries, so this is an idea that everybody should recognise. You'll notice that I begin this story with 'according to legend'. That's because NASA did consider using a pencil, but they decided against it because the lead would chip off and damage the instruments. I normally omit this detail to keep the story short.

Story 2: Alice in Wonderland

Do you remember this from Alice in Wonderland?

The Dodo begins a pompous long-winded speech:

"I move that the meeting adjourn, for the immediate adoption of more energetic remedies..."

...but suddenly the Eaglet cuts him off:

"Speak English! I don't know the meaning of half those long words, and I don't believe you do either!"

It's like that in our industry sometimes...

Story 3: KFC

Every few years the same story hits the news:

"Kentucky Fried Chicken is transporting its secret recipe to an undisclosed location via armed guard."

Supposedly, KFC keeps its top-secret chicken recipe in a bank vault, and only two executives have the key.

If you say so.

Obviously, it's a stunt. But the story generates a lot of PR for KFC because it plays on the widely-held belief that ideas are everything.

People believe that success is about coming up with one secret formula, one brilliant idea, one magic ingredient. In fact, raw ideas are usually worthless. I bet a food scientist could figure out the KFC recipe over the weekend.

What's important is how we execute those ideas, time and time again..

It's certainly true in our business...

Story 4: Centring the Saltshaker

A restaurant owner has a problem.

His staff drive him crazy because they don't listen to him and they constantly test his limits.

He's explaining all this to his mentor, New York steakhouse legend Pat Cecca, who eventually interrupts him:

> "Let me show you something. Take everything off this table, and leave the saltshaker by itself in the middle of the table."

The restaurant owner does as he's told.

Carefully, Cecca reaches out and slides the saltshaker a few centimetres off-centre.

> "Okay, now put the salt shaker back where it goes."

The restaurant owner puts it back in the middle of the table. But the second he does, Cecca reaches out and jabs it off-centre again.

> "Now put it back where you want it."

Again, the restaurant owner centres it. And again Cecca pushes it away. Finally, he reveals his point:

> "Listen, your staff and your guests are always moving your saltshaker off-centre. That's their job. It is the job of life! Your job is just to move the shaker back each time and let them know what excellence looks like. And if you're ever willing to let them decide where the centre is, then give up and toss them the keys to the whole damn restaurant!"

I think there's a great lesson here...

How to use this story
This is a good story to use with managers and team leaders. It reinforces their position as your organisation's centre of gravity, and helps them to see their role as guardians of your organisation's culture. It's also good when you're recovering from a knock. It lets you frame setbacks as natural, expected events.

Story 5: Lobster

Two hundred years ago, eating lobster was like eating a rat.

Eating lobster was considered such a 'cruel and unusual' punishment that several US states had laws against feeding it to prisoners.

Today lobster is a gourmet dish – one of the most expensive items on the menu.

A similar transformation is happening in our industry...

Story 6: Ferrari

In 1948, a peasant farmer started a business making tractors.

Within five years this man – Ferruccio – was one of the richest men in Italy. He amassed a fine collection of cars – Alfa Romeos, Maseratis, Lancias – but his heart belonged to his Ferraris, of which he owned six.

Just one thing bothered him: all of his Ferraris had clutch problems. One day in his workshop he discovered why: the clutch in his Ferraris was the same part he used in his tractors.

Ferruccio complained to Enzo Ferrari, who replied: "Ferruccio, you may be able to drive a tractor but you will never be able to handle a Ferrari properly."

Ferruccio was furious. He vowed to make a car worthy of beating a Ferrari. And as it happens, that's exactly what he did. He took his revenge by creating one of the most powerful, well renowned cars in the world.

The farmer's full name: Ferruccio Lamborghini.

your audience to dig deep and prove the doubters wrong!

Story 7: Angry Birds

In 2003, three students from Helsinki University started a video games company.

They made game after game, hoping that one would be successful. After six years they'd produced 51 titles, but none of them were hits.

For their 52nd game, they decided to make a simple puzzle physics game called Angry Birds.

Today their company – Rovio Entertainment – has over a billion users, 500 employees and annual revenue of over $200 million.

I love this story because it took them 51 failures to become a success.

It's a reminder of how...

How to use this story
Fairly obvious usage here. It's a 'stick with it' narrative to inspire teams that haven't been successful yet, and it's a good 'failure is good' message for people who need to turn over a lot of rocks before they find what they're looking for.

Story 8: Steve Jobs

Steve Jobs strolls into the employee break room one day in 1994 and starts making himself a bagel.

The staff chew warily. Suddenly, Jobs addresses everybody: "Who is the most powerful person in the world?"

Silence. A few names are proposed. Bill Clinton? Nelson Mandela? Then, Jobs erupts:

> "NO! You are ALL wrong. The most powerful person in the world is the storyteller. The storyteller sets the vision, values and agenda of an entire generation that is to come and Disney has a monopoly on the storyteller business."

He continues:

> "You know what? I am tired of that bullshit, I am going to be the next storyteller"

And out he walks with his bagel.

How to use this story
I found this encounter in a thread on Quora.com. It's a lovely scene that really engages an audience. You could use it get people hooked on storytelling. The fact that Steve Jobs held it in such regard helps people to recognise its importance.

Story 9: Finding Nemo

Finding Nemo was the biggest selling DVD in history.

Andrew Stanton tells the story of how he won the pitch to get it made. He walked into a meeting with Pixar boss John Lasseter tooled up with visual aids. He'd brought voiceover mock-ups and storyboards showing key plot points and story arcs.

Stanton pitched hard for over an hour – putting everything into bringing his script to life.

When it was over, Stanton collapsed into his chair and asked Lasseter what he thought. He replied:

"You had me at fish."

It's like that in our business. Smart people are often guilty of using a sledgehammer to crack a nut when they're desperate to get their point across.

> **How to use this story**
> You can use this story if you wish that your employees would present their ideas in a clear, straightforward way. It's a good reminder to get to the point.

Story 10: Any old map

A group of soldiers on a training exercise got lost in the Alps.

They were hungry and disoriented. They argued about which way to go, but in the fading light every peak looked the same.

The soldiers had no chance of surviving the night in the freezing temperatures.

Suddenly, a miracle. One of them found a map sewn into the lining of his kitbag. He plotted a route, and marched them briskly back to base.

Later, when they were warm and well fed, the soldier looked closer at his map. It was of the Pyrenees, hundreds of miles away. When you're lost, start walking.

> **How to use**
> This is a good story for when you want to create momentum, but you don't have all the answers. When you know the direction, but the exact destination still needs to be dialled in.

Story 11: New York

New York should have collapsed in 1980.

Over 130 years ago, the New York authorities held a conference to figure out how to manage the city's growth.

The experts agreed: it didn't look good.

The city was doubling in size every 10 years. By 1980 they predicted, you'd need six million horses to transport everybody. And those six million horse would produce so much crap that New York City was effectively doomed.

Obviously, things turned out differently. I love this story because it shows how people who make predictions for a living are hamstrung by the fact that they don't know what they don't know.

> **How to use this story**
> This story is a useful one when your success looks uncertain,or when you don't know what the future holds. It's a good story for encouraging followers to make a leap of faith.

Story 12: Iatrogenesis

Every year in the United States, 225,000 people die iatrogenic deaths.

According to the Journal of the American Medical Association, iatrogenesis is the third largest cause of death in the United States.

Iatrogenic. What is that word? Is it a disease, an accident, or something you get from smoking?

In fact, iatrogenic means inadvertent death caused by a doctor or a hospital. Why don't they just say that? Because it isn't exactly in medicine's best interests to put it in simple language that anybody can understand.

It's like that in our industry...

> **How to use this story**
> Usually when people use complex sentences and long words it's because they have something to hide. Audiences know this, so this is a good story to highlight the fact that you're 'telling it straight'.

How to use stories to simplify your presentations

Apparently, public speaking is the #1 fear.

No kidding. One of the worst experiences of my life was when I first stood up to speak in front of 200 people. I basically died.

This happened 10 years ago at a licensing industry conference. The organiser had casually invited me to speak, and I'd casually accepted. It was the first time I'd ever spoken in public, and I didn't think much of it until the day before the event. I'd watched plenty of people speak from the stage, and there didn't seem to be any special trick to it.

Thankfully, I remember little of what happened.

I do remember travelling on the train there, and having the inspired idea to jot down some bullet points on a scrap of paper.

I also remember the feeling of confidence I had, as they announced my name and I calmly walked through the crowd towards the stage.

And I definitely remember the 'oh shit' moment as I climbed up to the stage and saw all those faces looking up at me, expecting me to say something.

This wasn't what I'd imagined.

I thought it would be like a friendly chat. I'd say something, somebody else would say something, I'd reply with the answer. I had no idea that the 'social dynamics' are completely different when you stand up and speak to a group of people all at once.

I had no idea how totally alone you are: how if you ask a question, nobody will answer. How if you lose your thread or start to bomb, nobody will step in and take over. The audience will crash and burn with you.

I think I said a few sentences before I couldn't speak any more. I sort of gasped for air, I think, and made a few of those loud swallowing sounds that you make when you're really nervous and can't talk. Everybody knew I was corpsing, and they were just as embarrassed as I was.

It was awful. Since then I've spoken many times and it's never happened again. One of the main reasons it's never happened again is that I became serious about telling stories.

Today, the best way to put together a presentation or a talk is as a series of stories.

Stories are fantastic for public speaking. They are your 'secret weapon'. I know that's an overused term, but it's appropriate here.

Audiences never tire of hearing good stories

A few years ago I read an article about a research that had been conducted into jury persuasion. Apparently, if a lawyer needs to get an important issue firmly implanted into a jury's collective mind, he or she should try to link it with a well-known story.

The younger the age at which the jury members would have probably first heard it, the more effective it was probably going to be. Particularly effective were links to biblical parables, fables, nursery rhymes, and fairy stories.

Any time you plan to speak in public, the simplest and most engaging way to do it is to tell a sequence of short stories.

If you know five stories, you can speak anytime, anywhere

If you can tell five stories well, you can easily stand up and speak for half an hour or more - and hold everybody's attention too.

Imagine you tapped me on the shoulder while I was eating my breakfast one morning and led me into my garden where you'd assembled 250 strangers – all of whom were waiting to hear me speak for half an hour. There's a reasonable chance that I could pull it off. I wouldn't be amazing. But I definitely wouldn't die.

What's more, even if you wasn't kind enough to tell me anything about the people or why they were there, I'd still probably have a few stories that would resonate.

For example, in this book I've shared one about the lion tamer who figured out that lions freeze when you point a chair at them. They can't figure out which leg to swipe at first, so they do nothing. Show me one person who does't feel like that sometimes.

Then there's the story about NASA engineering a million dollar 'space pen', rather than using a pencil. That would probably work: there's not an industry on earth where people don't over engineer solutions.

Once you have a few powerful, flexible stories memorised, you can stand up and speak any time you like.

 Think of yourself as a DJ building a set. The stories are the records in your record box. All you have to do is choose the right ones, and play them in the right order.

Stories take care of the content, so you have more time to practise

Having the content nailed as a series of stories gives you more time to practise.

The reason most corporate presentations flop is because the presenter didn't practise. When most people stand up to deliver a talk, not only is the audience hearing their presentation for the first time – so are they.

Practise really is everything. I used to think that the advice you hear - "practice your speech or presentation out loud" – was just corny advice. Turns out, it's not.

People in business are fixated with PowerPoint. For most people, their PowerPoint document constitutes their entire presentation – their plan is to just stand up there and read it out.

I used to think this way. To me, preparing a presentation meant fiddling with my PowerPoint slide - getting the colours right, the animations just so. The minute I stepped out on stage, I realised that I'd worked on the wrong thing. They were looking at *me*, not the slides – and *I* liked like a nervous wreck.

 My friend Bob Etherington, who wrote the book Presentation Skills for Quivering Wrecks, says that back in the days of slide carousels he once saw a presenter accidentally run his slideshow 'back to front'. Not a single person in the audience noticed that what was on screen didn't match what he was saying.

Telling stories makes you look more prepared

Do you ever wonder how some people can speak for an hour without any notes? It's because they're working through a 'playlist' of stories they've memorised. If they did bring an outline of their presentation on paper, it would be six or seven bullet points at the most:

> So, I'll open with the one about Stevie Wonder and the Rolling Stones. Then the story about Sylvester Stallone and his struggle to get Rocky made, and then after that the story about Greg Norman self destructing on the last day of the US Masters.

It's very easy to learn a story. Once you've told it a few times it's locked away in your head. You don't need to write it down, and you certainly don't need a teleprompter.

You're more natural, and you connect with your audience much better.

> Using stories makes it easier to flex your presentation, too. If you need to make it longer, no problem – just add a couple of stories. Shorter? Same thing.

Final word

In the 1930s, Dr John Brinkley sold a 'miracle cure' for impotence. It involved transplanting goat testicles into men's scrotums.

The procedure didn't work. Brinkley would usually operate drunk, and maimed and killed a lot of his patients. His medical license was revoked, and the authorities took out full page advertisements in the *Journal of the American Medical Association*, warning the public not to deal with him.

None of this stopped Brinkley from becoming — for a time — one of America's wealthiest and most loved men. He was able to do this because he built an audience of his own, and nurtured it carefully with entertaining stories.

You see, Brinkley's patients did not read the *Journal of the American Medical Association*. What they did do was listen to the several radio stations that Brinkley controlled.

Every day, he would take to the airwaves and speak for hours on end to promote his goat gonad treatments. He'd tell colourful stories that chided impotent men, and cajoled their wives into buying his procedure. (His story is told in the book Charlatan, if you're interested.)

When you have an audience and you have stories that people want to hear, it's very difficult to stop you.

With an audience of your own, you can change things, you can sell things, you can get people to give you money to put goat parts in their testicles.

If people want to hear from you, good luck to anybody who gets in your way.

Thank you

BYE
BYE

Apparently, Amazon says that a product with bad reviews still sells better than a product with no reviews.

It would be great if you could leave me a review on Amazon. I ask because books that get no reviews never get recommended by Amazon's suggestion engine. They just sit there, alongside Piers Morgan's autobiography. So it would really help me if you could leave a review, to help others discover this book.

If you have any questions or comments that would help me make this book better, I'd love to hear from you.

My email address is **i.harris@gatehousegroup.co.uk**.

Thanks, Ian

/an :)

Ian Harris November 2014

Printed in Great Britain
by Amazon.co.uk, Ltd.,
Marston Gate.